BIG PICTURE PRESS
First published in the UK in 2023 by Big Picture Press,
an imprint of Bonnier Books UK
4th Floor, Victoria House
Bloomsbury Square, London WC1B 4DA
Owned by Bonnier Books
Sveavägen 56, Stockholm, Sweden
www.bonnierbooks.co.uk

1 3 5 7 9 10 8 6 4 2

ISBN 978-1-80078-464-2

This book was typeset in Eleonora Brush 2019 and Eleonora Pencil1.
The illustrations were created with acrylic paint, watercolour,
chalk, felt pens, collage and coloured digitally.

Edited by Joanna McInerney
Designed by Winsome d'Abreu and Melissa McInerney
Production by Ché Creasey

Printed in China

BUSY LITTLE FINGERS

ART

Eva Wong Nava
Eleonora Marton

BPP

HELL

Look around you.
Have you noticed that art is
EVERYWHERE?

Art is in your home.
Art is on the streets.
Art is on your TV.
Art is in France.
Art is in America.

O, ÁRT!

People
have been creating art
for hundreds of thousands of years.

Art helps us understand human stories and also to
know what was happening during a certain period of time.

Every piece of art has a story to tell.
In this book, our story begins in Italy.

ANDIAMO!
(This means 'let's go' in Italian.)

MANNERISM

Faces!
Beauty!
Vegetables?

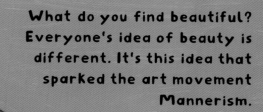

What do you find beautiful? Everyone's idea of beauty is different. It's this idea that sparked the art movement Mannerism.

Mannerism started about 500 years ago in Italy. The name of this art movement comes from the Italian word maniera which means 'MANNER' or 'style'. Mannerism was actually many different styles.

The Italian painter GIUSEPPE ARCIMBOLDO thought a big pear would make a nice nose. He decided to use vegetables and fruits to make people's faces, and even dared to make a delicious portrait of the Holy Roman Emperor Rudolf II! Luckily, the emperor saw the funny side.

WITHOUT BEING RUDE...

WHAT FRUITS AND VEGETABLES
CAN YOU USE TO CREATE A FACE?

WHY STOP AT VEGETABLES?

WHAT ELSE COULD YOU USE?

IMPRESS

Sunrise!
Outdoors!
Light!

Have you ever had the urge to take a photo
of something outside that you found impressive?

Many artists in France did just that, except instead
of taking a photo, they painted the environment
and people in new and exciting ways.

IONISM

That's what Impressionism is all about. It was born in France in the 1800s, and the father of Impressionism was **CLAUDE MONET**. He is famous for painting a picture of a sunrise called *Impression, Sunrise*. He loved working outside where he could watch how the sunlight changed the colours. He also loved how the breeze created movement.

Monet painted with broken lines and dabs of paint, making the pictures look blurry. An art critic laughed at Monet's impression of a sunrise, but instead of feeling sorry for himself, Monet called himself an Impressionist. And, just like that, an art movement was born.

IMPRESSED BY MONET?

GO OUTSIDE WITH A NOTEBOOK
AND USE LOTS OF DOTS, DASHES,
WIGGLES AND SQUIGGLES TO
CREATE YOUR OWN MASTERPIECE.

Do you like playing with building blocks? Two men in France did, and they ended up painting blocky pictures. This started an art movement called Cubism.

PABLO PICASSO and **GEORGES BRAQUE** created Cubism in the early 1900s. They wanted to make art look less flat and more 3D. This art movement quickly caught on. It inspired artists in Scotland, Europe and America to be more adventurous in creating.

If you like to combine letters and shapes, you're a cubist. If you like to make your squares look like blocks, you're a cubist.

And if you like seeing objects and people from different angles, you're a cubist.

17

HAS ALL THIS INSPIRED YOU?

THINK ABOUT WHAT YOU CAN DO
WITH YOUR BUILDING BLOCKS.

WHEN YOU CUT OUT DIFFERENT
SORTS OF PAPER AND GLUE THEM
TOGETHER TO MAKE PICTURES,
YOU'RE MAKING A COLLAGE.

FAUVISM

Wild!
Strokes!
Complementary
colours!

Do you like using bright colours to paint?
Two artists did. They were wild!

ANDRÉ DERAIN and
HENRI MATISSE were the
first Fauvists. They created
this style while they were
on holiday together. The sun
was bright and the colours
in the sea were brilliant.

When an art critic saw their work,
he jokingly said that both artists
were like 'wild beasts', or 'fauves'
in French, which gave the
movement its name.

Shh! The 's'
in fauves
is silent

Fauvism (pronounced 'foe-viz-um')
began in the early 1900s. The style
uses vibrant colours, and bold
brushstrokes. Fauvist painters loved to
squeeze paint from a tube directly onto their
canvasses, like toothpaste! They also liked to
make sure that they used colours that go side
by side with each other. These are called
'complementary colours'.

DO YOU FEEL LIKE BEING A WILD BEAST?

LET'S MAKE OUR OWN FAUVIST ART
WITH COMPLEMENTARY COLOURS.

23

SYMBOLISM

Emotions!
Mythology!
Dreams!

Do you ever have **GIGANTIC IDEAS?** You might have something really important to say. You might be feeling lonely, or happy, or in looovvve. But you might want to express these feelings as an idea or a story, to make other people feel what you are feeling.

Symbolism was developed first in French poetry in the late 1800s. Similar to how poetry uses words to express feelings, Symbolism uses art to express emotions. Symbolist artwork was often filled with mythical people and creatures.

Symbolism is not one style, but many. Artists such as **GUSTAV KLIMT** and **EDVARD MUNCH** are famous Symbolists. Both of these artists painted differently, but their artwork always makes you feel **SOMETHING.**

DO YOU FEEL LIKE EXPRESSING
YOUR EMOTIONS?

GLUE

CHOOSE AN OBJECT THAT YOU THINK
WOULD EXPRESS YOUR FEELINGS.

SOME PEOPLE FEEL EMOTIONS THROUGH COLOURS.
WHAT SHADE WOULD YOU USE TO PAINT HAPPINESS?

WHAT COLOUR MIGHT AN ANGRY BANANA BE?

27

SURRE

Free! Weird! Wonderful!

Does anyone feel sleepy around here? Surrealism is all about weird, dreamlike images like the ones swirling around in our heads. It's a little bit strange.

ALISM

A lobster on a telephone is Surrealism.
Doodles and squiggles on canvas is Surrealism.
Melting clocks in the desert is Surrealism.
RENÉ MAGRITTE was a Surrealist.
SALVADOR DALÍ was a Surrealist.

The person who thought
of the word 'surrealism' was
ANDRÉ BRETON, a French writer. If you
feel weirded out, don't worry, you're
not the only one. When Surrealism
first came to people's attention in the
1920s, not many people liked it.

But today, Surrealism is very
much part of our lives. Surrealism
is fun and it makes us laugh. It
makes us remember that life is
both real and dreamlike.

DO YOU FEEL LIKE CHANNELLING THE SURREALIST IN YOU?

LET'S PAINT A DREAM, JUST LIKE DALÍ.

Do you sometimes feel like you can't find the words to express how you're feeling? You might feel fuzzy and happy inside, like a big bowl of sunshine, or a bit confused, like a big bowl of spaghetti.

ABSTRAC

EXPRES

Rectangles!
Splashes!
Still and quiet!

Abstract Expressionism appeared in New York City during the 1940s and 50s. It is loud. It is quiet. It is a performance. Abstract Expressionism is hard to explain because it is all of these things. Abstract art is what some artists create when they can't find words to express their feelings.

JACKSON POLLOCK was an Abstract Expressionist. He is famous for throwing paint at his gigantic canvasses which he laid on the floor. His way of making art made him a performer, a bit like an actor in a show.

T
SIONISM

Let's put our hands together for **LEE KRASNER**. Her work is energetic and vibrant. She covered her canvasses with dashes, swirls and lines. People who talk about art say that Krasner's art is abstract and busy. Abstract means something you can't quite describe. It's an idea, but what is it REALLY?

DO YOU FEEL LIKE BEING

ABSTRACT ?

LET'S GET BUSY AND
EXPRESS OURSELVES LIKE
KRASNER DID.

POP ART

POP!

Do you like being popular? ANDY WARHOL did. He was a Pop Art artist. Pop Art means Popular Art. It is brash, colourful and revolutionary. Pop Art wants to go against what everyone thinks art is. Pop Art's message is:

GO BIG OR GO HOME

Pop Art can be videos, sculpture, music, boxes, collage and comics.

Advertising is Pop Art. Splashes of colour on a canvas is Pop Art. A short film with rock and roll music is Pop Art. An image repeated several times is Pop Art.

FIZZLE!

FLASH!

Pop Art started in the 1950s, when a few male artists wanted to make art more fun, more colourful, and more engaging. The only female Pop Art artist in the UK was PAULINE BOTY. Pauline's punchy work is a statement of girl power.

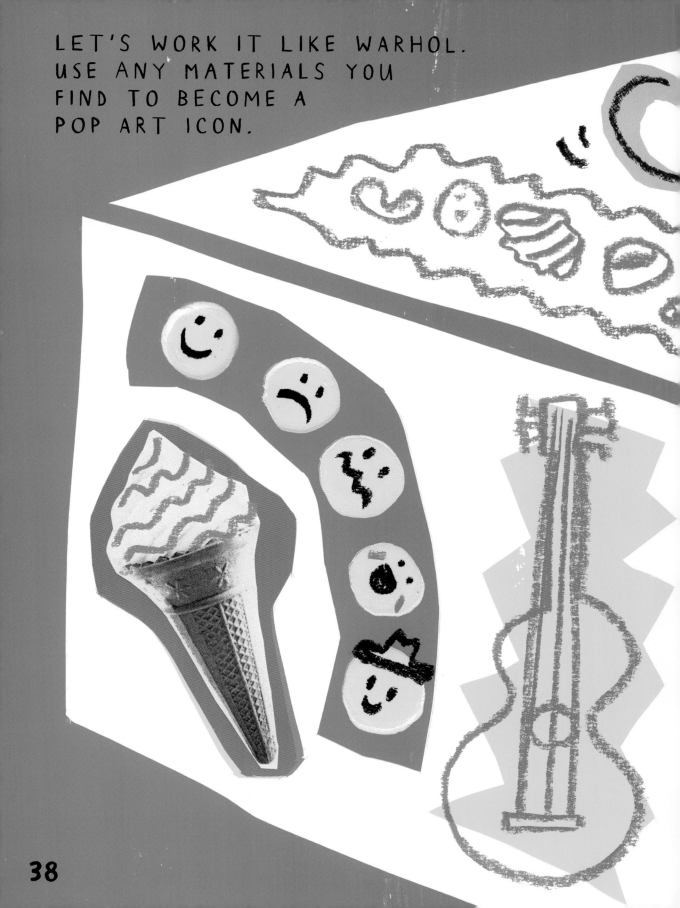

LET'S WORK IT LIKE WARHOL.
USE ANY MATERIALS YOU
FIND TO BECOME A
POP ART ICON.

39

OP ART

ILLUSIONS! OPTICAL! WHIRLS!

DID YOU KNOW THAT YOU CAN USE ART TO CAST SPELLS?

Sometimes, the way artists use colour and lines can create something mesmerising. They can trick you, and make you see things that maybe aren't really there at all!

OP ART OR OPTICAL ART WAS BORN IN THE 1960S IN GREAT BRITAIN.

You either love it or hate it. If you like geometrical shapes, you like Op Art. If you like swirls and whirls, you like Op Art. If you like optical illusions, then you also like Op Art.

BRIDGET RILEY IS KNOWN FOR HER CURVY BLACK AND WHITE LINES ON CANVAS.

Riley wants people to be open-minded about her work. The more you focus on her lines, the more things you begin to see.

LET'S SNAP OUT OF IT AND CREATE OUR OWN...

42

OPTICAL
ART.

CONTEM

Dots! Pumpkins! Repeat!

Contemporary art is happening right **NOW** — while you read this book!

Contemporary art is not a movement, but a name given to art that is being created by artists who are still alive.

Contemporary art is not one style — it is many. It can be paintings, videos and installations. Installations are pieces made up of sculptures or objects put together in an open space.

PORARY ART

YAYOI KUSAMA is a contemporary artist. She was born in 1929 in Matsumoto, Japan. She is still creating art. Her work is iconic. This means that you can't mistake it for anything else. In fact, Kusama herself is a piece of art with her flaming-orange hair and polka-dotted outfits. Kusama loves polka dots so much that she puts them everywhere. She also loves pumpkins. Sometimes these pumpkins are plastered with polka dots! Dots, dots, dots, everywhere.

Feeling a bit
D O T T Y ?

Let's make art
like Kusama.

46

47

MAKE YOUR MARK!

Art movements come and go, but they will always be remembered as long as there are artworks to remind us of who the artists were and what they were part of. Artworks become part of history. They help us understand why artists painted the way they did. Let your pieces of art become part of art history too.

OUR STORY DOESN'T END HERE...
ART WILL ALWAYS BE IN THE MAKING!